Century Hutchinson New Zealand Ltd.
An imprint of the Century Hutchinson Group.
32-34 View Road, P.O. Box 40-086, Glenfield, Auckland 10.

Century Hutchinson Ltd.
62-65 Chandos Place, Covent Garden, London WC2N 4NW.

Century Hutchinson Australia Pty. Ltd.
16-22 Church Street, Hawthorn, Melbourne, Victoria 3122.
89-91 Albion Street, Surry Hills, Sydney, N.S.W. 2010.

Century Hutchinson South Africa Pty. Ltd.
P.O. Box 337, Bergvlei 2012, South Africa.

First published 1987

Printed in Hong Kong

ISBN 0 09 172750 2

THE MAGPIES

WRITTEN by
Denis GLOVER

PICTURES by
Dick FRIZZELL

AND QUARDLE DODLE
ARDLE WARDLE DOODLE
THE MAGPIES SAID

AND QUARDLE OODLE
ARDLE WARDLE DOODLE
THE MAGPIES
SAID

AND QUARDL
ARDLE WARD
THE MAGPIE

AND QUARDLE
ARDLE WARDLE
THE MAGPIES

JODLE
DOODLE
SAY